Our Catholic Life

A READING AND STUDY GUIDE FOR ADULT FAITH FORMATION

3

✦ CREED ✦

DRAWING CLOSER TO CHRIST

Bill Huebsch

TWENTY-THIRD PUBLICATIONS

twentythirdpublications.com

IMPRIMATUR

✝   Most Reverend Joseph R. Binzer
    Auxiliary Bishop
    Archdiocese of Cincinnati
    February 9, 2016

The *Imprimatur* ("Permission to Publish") is a declaration that a book or pamphlet is considered to be free of doctrinal or moral error. It is not implied that those who have granted the *Imprimatur* agree with the contents, opinions, or statements expressed.

Twenty-Third Publications
1 Montauk Avenue, Suite 200, New London, CT 06320
(860) 437-3012 » (800) 321-0411 » www.twentythirdpublications.com

ISBN: 978-1-62785-170-1
Library of Congress Catalog Card Number: 2016939658
Printed in the U.S.A.

Contents

How to use this study guide in seven small-group sessions

Gather. As people arrive for each session, welcome them warmly and offer them refreshments. You may wish to have sacred music playing to set the tone. If people are new to each other, name tags can help break the ice. When everyone has arrived, gather your group and invite them to open their books to today's material.

Begin with *Lectio divina* prayer. Each session opens with a short and prayerful reflection on a scriptural text that is found in that section of the *Catechism*. Here are the steps:

1. Begin with the Sign of the Cross.

2. Read aloud the Introduction for this session.

3. Call everyone to prayer using these or similar words: *Let us turn our hearts to Christ now and hear the word of the Lord.*

4. Invite a member of the group to proclaim the Scripture we present for you.

5. Invite your group members to share about the text, first in twos and threes if you wish, and then as a whole group. Sharing: *What word or phrase in this reading catches your ear? What is God saying to us in this scriptural text?*

6.   Now pray in these or similar words:
O God, we know that you are with us and that you behold all we are about to do. Now grant that, by the power of the Holy Spirit, we might be faithful as we study our faith and charitable in how we treat each other. Through Christ, our Lord. Amen.

Read. Moving around the circle in your group and rotating readers, read aloud each numbered faith statement. Group members should note items in the material that strike them as especially important. Do not read aloud the **We Believe** statements. They are provided as an enhancement to the text.

Group or personal process. When you come to the process notes, pause to continue around the circle, discussing as the notes direct. Use our suggestions as a starting point, and add your own questions, prayers, or action plans.

Finish. As you conclude this session, call everyone to prayer once again. Reread the scriptural text we used in the beginning. Then move around the circle one last time to share: *In light of this reading and what we have learned today, what has touched you most deeply? What new insight of faith will you carry away from here? What new questions about faith have arisen for you? How will today's discussion work its way into your daily life?* Close your session with the prayer we provide, or lead a spontaneous prayer in which everyone shares their own prayer.

Session One

BASED ON ARTICLES 422–451 AND 456–478 OF THE *CATECHISM OF THE CATHOLIC CHURCH*. TO READ A SUMMARY OF THIS SECTION, SEE *CATECHISM* ARTICLES 452–455 AND 479–483

Introduction

No study of the Catholic faith would be complete without a long look at the one around whom we gather: the person of Jesus Christ. The name Jesus means "God saves," and in this part of our work we will consider what that means to us personally and communally. The title "Christ" means "Anointed One" or Messiah. In a sense, we all share in the anointing of Christ: we are also priest, prophet, and king. And yet Jesus Christ is true God and true man, in the unity of his divine person, God incarnate. As we come to understand what the Incarnation means for us and the world, we will find that it is the mystery of the wonderful union of the divine and human natures in the one person of the Word.

Scripture

READER: A reading from the Gospel of Mark.

Jesus went on with his disciples to the villages of Caesarea Philippi; and on the way he asked his disciples, "Who do people say that I am?" And they answered him, "John the Baptist; and others, Elijah; and still others, one of the prophets." He asked them, "But who do you say that I am?" Peter answered him, "You are the Messiah." (MARK 8:27–29)

PART ONE ✦ *ARTICLES 422–429 OF THE CATECHISM*

The good news

[1] He was born of a Jewish woman, a daughter of Israel named Mary of Nazareth. It was during the time of King Herod the Great and the emperor Caesar Augustus. He was a carpenter by trade, "Joseph's son," according to those who knew him.

[2] He taught in public and in private, and he once said between the cradle and the cross, "Love one another as I have loved you."

[3] He died in Jerusalem some thirty years later, crucified and essentially alone save a few women and one or two brave men; this happened under the hand of the procurator Pontius Pilate during the reign of the emperor Tiberius.

[4] We believe that this man we are describing here, Jesus Christ, is the eternal Son of God. We believe that this man is, in the words of the opening chapter of John's gospel, "the Word made flesh" who "lived among us" and whose glory we have seen.

[5] We believe that this man is "full of grace and truth," from whose "fullness we have all received grace: grace upon grace." We believe that, while the law came through Moses, "grace and truth came through Jesus Christ."

[6] When we speak of "passing on the faith" from one generation to the next, it is this faith of which we speak. The early disciples burned with this faith, with a desire to pass on to others knowledge of the one whom they had seen with their own eyes, their teacher and the one whom they had touched: Jesus Christ.

[7] We give a name to the passing on of faith when we echo it in our lives and share it with others as a witness. We call it "catechesis," a Greek word that means "to echo."

*We pass on our faith, one to another, in a process called **catechesis**. In this process we live convincingly and echo the faith in our lives and words. At the heart of all catechesis is the person of Jesus Christ.*

[8] Saint John Paul II published a historic document on catechesis very early in his papacy. It is called, in Latin, *Catechesi Tradendae* and, in English, *On Catechesis in our Time.* In article 6 of this document he describes how we pass on our faith: "Christ, the Incarnate Word and Son of God...is taught—everything else is taught with reference to him—and it is Christ alone who teaches—anyone else teaches to the extent that he [or she] is Christ's spokesperson, enabling Christ to teach with his [or her] lips. . . Every catechist should be able to apply to himself [or herself] the mysterious words of Jesus: 'My teaching is not mine, but his who sent me.'"

[9] Catechesis is the process within the Church through which we echo this faith from generation to generation. At the very heart of all catechesis we find, not a book or a theological system or a litany

of doctrine and dogma or a list of rules and regulations, but a *person*, and that person is Jesus of Nazareth.

Group or personal process

- How have you met Christ in your own life?

- How do you experience your own daily walk with Christ?

- Read faith statement #5 again: we believe that grace comes to us through Christ. How does grace empower you to live with the forgiveness, generosity, mercy, and love of Christ?

- To whom are you sent as a catechist? To whom are you sent to echo your faith?

PART TWO ✛ **ARTICLES 430–451 OF THE *CATECHISM***
Who do we say he is?

[10] "Jesus." In Hebrew the name means "God saves." And indeed, through Jesus and through his life, death, and resurrection, God is saving us and bringing all of salvation history into one shining moment. Human sinfulness, that inclination to reject God, is forgiven, and we are made whole again.

[11] This is a holy name that summons for us the image of God. The name of Jesus is at the heart of all our prayer, concluding, as we often do, in these words: "through Christ our Lord. Amen."

[12] The name Christ is a Greek title that means "Messiah." In Hebrew it carries the meaning "anointed." And indeed, Jesus

Christ is the anointed one of God, the one who announces the reign of God.

[13] Anointed by the Spirit in the river, anointed by God on the mountain, Jesus Christ is the Messiah. He was of royal family ties, born as a descendent of King David. His teaching and his many works made clear that he was the holy one of God.

WE BELIEVE

Jesus is the Christ, the anointed one of God. He is the one who was to come, the Messiah, the object of all our hope. There is no other name under heaven by which we will be saved.

[14] As Luke's gospel retells it in chapter 4, he came to Nazareth as a young man, to the synagogue on the Sabbath; standing to read, he was handed the scroll of the prophet Isaiah. He unrolled the scroll with great purpose, found the passage he wanted, and read aloud for all to hear.

[15] "The Spirit of the Lord is upon me," he read, "because he has anointed me to bring good news to the poor..." His audience was stunned! And within hours or perhaps days at the most, the work of teaching and healing had begun.

[16] From almost the beginning, it seems, Jesus understood the dangerous work to which he was called. For when you announce the reign of God, you must at the same time announce the end of darkness.

[17] In your very person, you become a servant, a person of tremendous mercy and love, and a forgiver. In a word, you prepare to die to yourself in love, and only that, you realize, will lead to joy, glory,

and resurrection. Jesus offered his life to liberate us, and this great act of love opened the reign of God for all.

[18] Son of God: the title is given to angels in the Old Testament, to the chosen people, to the children of Israel, and even to their kings. But for Peter it is a different story. He names Jesus as the Christ, the Messiah, and the Son of God. And Jesus assures Peter that this insight into his divinity came from "my Father who is in heaven," according to Matthew's gospel, chapter 16, verse 17.

WE BELIEVE

Jesus is true God and truly human in the unity of his divine person. These two natures are not confused but are unified in God's Son. Jesus is Lord.

[19] Jesus is also called Son of God. St. Paul, after his conversion and while still in Damascus, within days of having met the Lord, is already proclaiming about Jesus, "He is the Son of God," in Acts, chapter 9, verse 21.

[20] At Jesus' baptism in Matthew's gospel, chapter 3, it was the very voice of God who proclaimed, "This is my Son, the Beloved…"

[21] And later in this same gospel (chapter 17) we hear that voice again, this time high on a mountain, saying "This is my Son, the Beloved…" In the words of the guard at Jesus' cross later again in this same gospel, in chapter 27, we ourselves now proclaim, "Truly this man was God's Son!" "Lord."

[22] The people of the Old Testament did not utter God's name, which was revealed to Moses on Horeb as YHWH. They revered it too much to say it aloud. Instead, they used the name "Lord," rendered in Greek, *Kyrios*. The people of the New Testament also used the title "Lord" with reference to the same God but also—and this is new—with reference to Jesus.

[23] The title suggests an intimacy, recognition of divine presence, yes, but closeness reserved for friends. Hence, at that famous fish fry on the beach in the Gospel of John, Peter finally recognizes Christ and utters, "It is the Lord!" He was referring to the friend whom he had earlier betrayed.

[24] When we give Christ the title "Lord," we give him honor, glory, and praise. Indeed, there is no power in heaven or on earth greater than that of the presence of the risen Lord among us. In this power, offered to us all, we become other Christs ourselves. In our liturgies, we announce this as a blessing: "The Lord be with you." "And with your spirit."

Group or personal process

- What do you believe about Jesus? Who is he in your life?

- How do you pray with Jesus on a daily basis?

- How is Jesus "Lord" in your life? How do you relate to Jesus as Lord?

Jesus is born

[25] The story of the birth of Jesus is a story of love. It has love at its beginning and love at its end. Down through the centuries, God had expressed love for us humans. In a thousand various ways this love was communicated to us.

[26] Now, in the birth of Jesus Christ, love would become fully human. Mary's blessed willingness to say "yes" to God paved the way for this. By the grace offered through Christ, God would make it possible for us to return to Paradise; God made it possible for us to live as his children again and to become sons and daughters of God!

[27] The text of the New Testament gushes with this love! Look at the First Letter of John, chapter 4. "God's love was revealed among us in this way," the text says in verse 9; "God sent his only Son into the world so that we might live through him."

[28] Or the Gospel of John, chapter 3, verse 16: "For God so loved the world that he gave his only Son…"

[29] Christ is our model of holiness, teaching us to be humble, to follow him on the Way. It can all be summed up in this command from John's gospel: "Love one another as I have loved you." Christ also gives us a share in the divine life. The Son of God became human, as St. Thomas Aquinas taught, so that we humans might become gods.

Incarnation

[30] We give a name to the fact that God became human, and that name is "Incarnation." There is great mystery in this: The great di-

vine being, the supernatural source of love and life, takes on human nature without losing the divine nature, in order to teach us to love, to heal our wounded souls, and to make us whole again. And the style of this ministry toward us was complete humility.

[31] Belief in the Incarnation is essential to our faith, of course. Over the years, various believers in the Church have wandered into misunderstandings about this. Some have argued that Jesus was human but not divine. Some that Jesus was divine but not human. Some that Jesus was part one and part the other but not quite fully both.

WE BELIEVE

The Incarnation is the mystery of the wonderful union of the divine and human natures of Christ in the one person who is the light of the world.

---

[32] We believe that Jesus is truly human and truly divine at one and the same time. We believe that the divinity and humanity of Christ is inseparable, true, and complete.

[33] The *Constitution on the Church in the Modern World* from Vatican II offers us a helpful reflection on this. "The Son of God," it says in article 22, "has in a certain way united himself with each individual. He worked with human hands, he thought with a human mind. He acted with a human will, and with a human heart he loved. Born of the Virgin Mary, he has truly been made one of us, like to us in all things except sin."

[34] Christ had a human soul and was endowed with human knowledge. Hence, that knowledge was not itself without limits. Christ lived in a period of history, in a given part of the world. He learned

about human life through experience, and he did this voluntarily. He loved us with a human heart, loved us to the end.

[35] And he had no conflict between his divine will, on the one hand, and his human will, on the other. Listening to his own heart, Jesus followed the way set before him. His body was finite, as are our human bodies, but we love to gaze on the face of Christ; and when we venerate his image, it is actually the Lord himself whom we adore.

Group or personal process

- How do you experience closeness with Jesus Christ? How do you identify with him?

- Write out in a few lines your own central beliefs about Jesus Christ. Match this against the Apostles' or Nicene Creeds that we pray as Church. What is affirmed for you? How are you challenged?

Prayer

Jesus, we believe in you. Help our unbelief. You have shown us the way we should walk as your disciples. As we struggle to follow you faithfully on our journeys of faith, send your Sprit into our hearts so that we can understand more fully your mercy, forgiveness, and love. Help us become more and more a faithful witness to you in the world. We pray in your holy name, Amen.

Session Two

BASED ON ARTICLES 484–507 AND 963–972 OF THE *CATECHISM OF THE CATHOLIC CHURCH*. TO READ A SUMMARY OF THIS SECTION, SEE *CATECHISM* ARTICLES 508–511 AND 973–975

Introduction

Having been introduced to Jesus Christ in the last session, we turn now to meet Mary, his mother. Mary is important to us Christians because she is the first disciple. With Joseph, her husband, she was Jesus' first teacher, model of love, and mother. Mary is truly "Mother of God." The Greek word that expresses this is *Theotokos*. With her whole being, Mary is "the handmaid of the Lord." By pronouncing her "fiat" or "yes" at the Annunciation and giving her consent to the Incarnation, Mary was already collaborating with the whole work her Son was to accomplish. Mary is now with God, where she already shares in the glory of her Son's resurrection, anticipating the resurrection of all. We pray with Mary so that we can draw closer to Christ in our own lives.

Scripture

READER: A reading from the Gospel of Luke.

When Elizabeth heard Mary's greeting, the child leaped in her womb. And Elizabeth was filled with the Holy Spirit and exclaimed with a loud cry, "Blessed are you among women, and blessed is the fruit of your womb." (LUKE 1:41–42)

PART ONE ✠ **ARTICLES 484–494 OF THE CATECHISM**

Born of the Virgin Mary

[1] What happened to Mary of Nazareth, how it happened, and when it happened are great mysteries that are known only by faith. Mary of Nazareth was a holy woman who desired the presence of the divine. She listened to God's word and gave her consent to God's invitation to bear Jesus. The Holy Spirit gave her assurance, strength, and the miraculous conception of Jesus.

[2] And even though it was indeed Christ the anointed one of God whom she conceived, the realization of that by others occurred only gradually and progressively: shepherds in one account, magi in another, John the Baptist, the disciples, and us.

[3] What we Catholics believe about Mary derives directly from what we believe about Christ. Our devotion to Mary is meant always and only to lead us to deeper devotion to Christ, her son.

[4] We believe Mary conceived this child, having given her full consent to the divine invitation. We believe Mary had been chosen by God for this. In a sense, she is a "new Eve," a new mother for a new people, the People of God in Christ.

[5] There were many holy women in the story of salvation history, and Mary stands as the culminating player. We begin with Eve, who,

along with Adam her husband, was disobedient, and yet God promised she would be the mother of all living people; then there were Sarah and Rebecca; Hannah, the mother of Samuel; and Deborah, a great judge in Israel; there were Ruth and Naomi, whose fidelity was legendary; there was Judith, who trusted her own intuition and won the day; and there was Esther, who prevented genocide by her intervention; and many others.

The Immaculate Conception

[6] We believe that Mary was "full of grace," in the words of the angel Gabriel. We refer to the moment when Mary learned that she would become pregnant and be overshadowed by the power of the Most High as her "annunciation." It was announced to her that God had found favor with her; God had graced her with love.

[7] There is no doubt that God had chosen to give himself generously to this young woman. The Church has meditated on this reality down through the centuries and come to believe with certainty that Mary was not subject in her life to that inclination that we call "original sin."

[8] We believe that from the moment of her own conception in the womb of her mother, Mary was full of grace. We give a name to this freedom from sin that Mary enjoyed. We call it the Immaculate Conception.

[9] Mary is not the Lord, but she is the Mother of the Lord. Nonetheless, we believe the Holy Spirit prepared Mary for her generous role in the history of salvation by communicating God to her so fully that Mary's own heart was made pure. She was free of sin. We share this faith with Christians of the Eastern tradition, who call Mary "the All-Holy," and with many other Christian churches.

[10] And Mary responded to God only as one so full of God's power could. She said "Yes." Without fully understanding but with complete trust in God whom she loved, she spoke those immortal words recorded in Luke, chapter 1, verse 38: "Here I am, the servant of the Lord; let it be with me according to your word." This consent was full, free, and generous; Mary was accepting her role in the mystery of redemption.

Group or personal process

- Think back over your life to difficult and complex decisions you have faced, such as entering religious life, getting married, becoming pregnant, accepting a new job, or making other major changes. How did you sense the call of God in those moments?

- What role does Mary have in your own spiritual journey?

- How does Mary lead you to draw closer to Christ?

Mary, ever virgin

[11] We believe that Mary gave birth to Jesus who was God's only Son, and therefore we give her the title Mother of God.

[12] Indeed, when Mary went to visit her cousin Elizabeth, the mother of John the Baptist, Elizabeth was stirred by the Holy Spirit, according to the text of Luke. "How fortunate I am!" she proclaimed, "that the mother of my Lord comes to visit me!" We refer to this visit by the two cousins as the "Visitation."

[13] We believe that Mary conceived Jesus only by the power of the Holy Spirit, just as we must all "conceive" Jesus in our own hearts by that very same power. This virginal conception was an early belief in the Christian community and is a sign that Jesus truly was "Son of God."

[14] The prophet Isaiah had given a divine promise in chapter 7, verse 14: "Look, the young woman is with child and shall bear a son, and shall name him Immanuel." This is a mystery that points to the great reality of God's unending love and God's commitment to us.

[15] We can only understand what her virginity means with eyes of faith. Indeed, it is a great expression of faith that Jesus was born of the Holy Spirit and that Mary gave such full consent to God's plan. It is a sign of Mary's undivided heart regarding the love of God in her life and in all our lives!

[16] Participation in the divine life, after all, is the power to become children of God, as John's gospel attests in chapter 1. Such children of God, he says, are "born, not of blood, or of the will of the flesh, or of the will of humans, but of God." Mary demonstrates for us what it means to be as God's own spouse.

[17] Mary is virgin because her virginity is a sign of her faith, which is what enabled her to conceive. Mary is blessed not because she bore Christ but because she believed in him with all her heart. We will be blessed like that too. Like all of us human beings, Mary also needed to be redeemed by Christ.

WE BELIEVE

With her whole being, Mary is the handmaid of the Lord. She remained ever a virgin.

[18] The great *Constitution on the Church* from Vatican II includes a chapter on Mary. There we read in article 63: "The Son whom she brought forth is he whom God placed as the first-born among many children, that is, the faithful in whose generation and formation she cooperates with a mother's love." Mary's spiritual motherhood extends, therefore, to all people whom Christ loves.

Group or personal process

- How can reverence for Mary lead you closer to the Lord?

- Mary's willingness to trust in God and follow God's call changed the world! How is your call to discipleship similar?

Mother of the Church

[19] We Catholics understand Mary to be the Mother of the Church, that is, of all who believe in Christ. Mary was united with Christ as mother is to son, and in the same way she is united to the Church because we are all in Christ. From the cradle to the cross Mary was present in Christ's life, and so she is in our own.

[20] Even after Jesus' death, resurrection, and ascension, Mary associated with the apostles, held all these things in her heart, and remained faithful throughout. We believe that Mary remains joined to Christ forever, sharing in the heavenly banquet.

WE BELIEVE

Mary was taken up body and soul into the glory of heaven. We believe that Mary continues to exercise her maternal love on behalf of all Christians.

[21] We believe she lives now in glory, raised up by God who first chose her and revealed to her the divine plan for salvation. We give her the title "Queen of Heaven" because we believe so fervently that she shares in her Son's resurrection. We give this belief a name: Mary's "Assumption."

Our Mother too

[22] Mary is a unique member of the Church because of her unique role in the divine plan of salvation. It is fitting and right, therefore, for us to give her reverence and for us to copy her faith as our own: her obedience and her burning charity.

[23] We experience Mary as a means of grace and a means of divine light that guides us in our spiritual journey. We give her reverence and honor and, in doing so, we give her the titles of Advocate, Helper, Benefactress, and Mediatrix.

[24] We are careful to mention, however, that Mary's unique role for us does not diminish the role of Christ. Christ is Lord, and Christ alone.

Hail Mary!

[25] Because of her important role, the Church honors Mary with devotion. All devotion to Mary honors Christ and leads to Christ. Indeed, in the words of Mary's great song, recorded in Luke, chapter 1, verse 48, "Surely, from now on all generations will call me blessed!"

[26] Mary uttered these words not to bring praise to herself but to express the tremendous blessing it was for her to have been chosen for this mission. Likewise for us: when we devote ourselves to Mary, when we revere her, it is because of the tremendous blessing it is for us to know Christ.

[27] In looking to Mary, we in the Church see ourselves. We hear her words, "I am here." We recall her great trust, her journey of faith, and her unity with Christ.

[28] In a real sense, Mary is an image of the whole Church gathered as we are from all the earth, receiving grace through Christ and becoming always more the persons we are created to be.

[29] And like Mary, when grace presents itself to us and we hear the divine voice calling us to follow the Word of God, let us say with Mary: "I am here for whatever you desire of me."

Group or personal process

- When you pause to hear God speaking in your life, as Mary did at the time of the Annunciation, what do you hear God calling you to be or to become?

- Read faith statements #27–29 again. In what times of your life have you been called to say "I am here" or to say "Yes" to God, even when it was difficult to do so?

Prayer

Hail Mary, full of grace, the Lord is with you. Blessed are you among women, and blessed is the fruit of your womb, Jesus. Holy Mary, Mother of God, pray for us sinners, now and at the hour of our death. Amen.

Session Three

BASED ON ARTICLES 512–560 OF THE *CATECHISM OF THE CATHOLIC CHURCH*. TO READ A SUMMARY OF THIS SECTION, SEE *CATECHISM* ARTICLES 561–570

Introduction

It is time now to turn to consider the life of Jesus, how he taught, healed, and prayed. We know that the whole of Christ's life was a continual teaching: his silences, his miracles, his gestures, his prayer, his love for people, his special affection for the little and the poor, his way of the cross, and his resurrection. He was the master catechist of all time. In his teaching, Jesus announced the reign of God and called us to follow in his footsteps. Jesus fulfilled the law with such perfection that he revealed its ultimate meaning, mysterious as that is. We too are called to live out the paschal mystery as Christ did.

Scripture

READER: A reading from the Gospel of Mark.

The apostles gathered around Jesus, and told him all that they had done and taught. He said to them, "Come away to a deserted place all by yourselves and rest a while." For many were coming and going, and they had no leisure even to eat. And they went away in the boat to a deserted place by themselves. Now many saw them going and recognized them, and they hurried there on foot from all the towns and arrived ahead of them. As he went ashore, he saw a great crowd; and he had compassion for them, because they were like sheep without a shepherd; and he began to teach them many things. (**MARK 6:30–34**)

READER: The word of the Lord.

ALL: Thanks be to God.

The life of Jesus of Nazareth

[1] In a sense, there's a lot we don't know about Jesus of Nazareth. The gospels are our chief source of knowledge about him; even though four of them are in the Bible, really there is only *one* gospel with *four* traditions.

[2] The gospels are not a biographical account; even if they were, they omit many years of Jesus' life. In the years of his life that they cover, they omit many details. We're curious about this because of the importance that we attach to Jesus, but we'll never really know a lot about him.

[3] What we do know is found mainly in the gospels, where the authors were careful to make sure that their readers would grasp the greater reality behind their accounts. The gospels are full of symbols, therefore, such as the swaddling clothes at his birth, the journey to Jerusalem, and the many signs and wonders of Jesus' ministry.

[4] The gospel writers were people of faith, first and foremost, eager to share what they had heard and seen. Looking back at his life some thirty or forty years later, which is when these gospels were written, the writers were able to understand more clearly than at the time of his death. Distance from a profound event gives us perspective.

[5] To them, every aspect of Jesus' life was revelation: whether words or deeds or prayer or feasting or resting in silence...In the end, his whole life was about the paschal mystery. He committed himself in love to those around him, especially to the poor and rejected, and from that love, all who knew him experienced freedom.

[6] The goal of his ministry was to restore to the human race the possibility of "living in Paradise." It isn't so much that the Father was demanding the bloody sacrifice of his own son in order to be appeased for our wrongdoing. That sounds like the gods of the ancients but not like the God of Jesus.

[7] It is more likely this: that we were created for love, which entails that we die to ourselves. But we had lost our way and chosen to be selfish instead. In the great cosmic scheme of things the human race had lost sight of the reign of God. By his actions on the cross, his tremendous act of love and forgiveness, Christ reopened for us that spiritual way that had been closed.

[8] He announced the reign of God to us and, through this act, along with all the works and teachings throughout his lifetime, he restored us to the pathways of love. We have a name for this central mystery of Christ's life and work. We refer to it as "the paschal mystery."

[9] By it we refer to his self-giving life, death, and resurrection. We sum this up in our liturgy when we proclaim, "By your Cross and Resurrection, you have set us free..."

Example

[10] Christ provides an example for us, a model of one living the paschal mystery. We are invited to follow him, to take up our own cross and become humble as he did, become poor as he did, and die to ourselves as he did. By his grace and his grace alone we are able to live as his followers and become members of his body.

Group or personal process

- How do you live the paschal mystery in your own life? In other words, how do you practice self-giving love for the good of others?

- How do you "die in Christ"? What experiences of "new life" have you had?

- How do you address Jesus in prayer? What is the nature of your relationship with him when you turn to him in your quiet and prayerful moments?

The long wait

[11] When we speak of God's Son "coming to earth from heaven," we do not mean to suggest that he came to earth from some other physical place, like from another planet or another country.

[12] Christ is the Son of God but not in the biological sense that you are a son or daughter of your parents. We use our feeble language to express a much greater truth.

[13] Down through the centuries, we waited and God promised. Promised what? Promised that love would return, that full human life would be possible, that we would again live as we were created to, and that we would draw near to God again.

[14] All through this time, God was preparing us to receive this "bursting forth of a new dawn" that would occur in Jesus. This new dawn occurred in the birth of Jesus to that humble and willing woman, Mary, and to her loving husband, Joseph. It happened, not as a whirlwind, nor as an earthquake, nor as a great fire, but in a child's cry.

[15] What all the prophets had foretold was now reality. St. John the Baptist was the last of those prophets, only a few months older than Jesus himself. He brings the period of waiting to a conclusion and makes the final preparation to help us "prepare the way of the Lord."

[16] During Advent each year, we revisit that long period of waiting for Christ to appear and the energy of love to be restored.

The Christmas mystery

[17] Jesus was born into poverty, a family that could not find lodging on a cold, Middle Eastern winter night. And we, too, it seems, must become childlike in order to enter the reign of God. For only when Christ is formed in us will the mystery of Christmas be achieved.

The infancy

[18] He was a Jew and remained one throughout his life. He was circumcised in the Jewish ceremony and then presented in the temple as a firstborn son would be.

[19] Later, there was a mysterious moment in his childhood, one retold in the Gospel of Matthew although omitted from other gospels. People of great wisdom called "magi" came in faith to welcome Christ and to celebrate this mystery. The message was clear: God welcomes all to know Christ. We call the feast that commemorates this event "the Epiphany."

[20] For most of Jesus' childhood and adolescent years we are given very few details. We know he lived at home with his parents, worked as a carpenter alongside his father, and, at age twelve, visited the temple with them. In telling this story later, the gospel writer provides a prequel to the passion: he was "lost" for three days, then "found," the story tells us, saying he was doing his Father's work.

Baptism

[21] By the time of his baptism, Jesus, it seems, had begun to come to terms with his mission. John's baptism was "of repentance for the forgiveness of sins" but Jesus insists on entering into the waters and, upon leaving them, had his own epiphany.

[22] It was during a period of prayer, according to Luke, in chapter 3, verse 21 and 22, that Jesus heard the heavenly voice: "You are my Son, the Beloved; with you I am well pleased."

[23] Jesus will be the source of this divine blessing for all of humanity. Soon we will all see ourselves as sons and daughters of God, knowing that great joy of being loved, of being "like God." In this moment of baptism, it all begins for Jesus: the clear mandate of God, the work of healing and teaching and loving, the journey to the cross, and the resurrection to new life.

[24] And for us Christians, our own work begins at baptism too: the clear mandate of God, the work of healing and teaching and loving, the journey to the cross, and the resurrection to new life.

Temptations

[25] Then he retreated to the desert wilderness to prepare himself for the work before him. Tempted like all humans are to selfishness, greed, and unilateral power, he resisted. He remained faithful to the plan of salvation willed by his Father.

[26] Jesus, it would turn out later, never gave up his love. He surrendered all else: daily comfort, a permanent household life, public acceptance, and even his own life, but *never his love.*

[27] Understanding this is the key to understanding Christ. This desert retreat was the beginning but it would not be the end for him. Each Lent when we repeat this forty-day desert retreat, we are offered the chance to begin again ourselves.

Group or personal process

- What would it take for you to make this commitment: "I'll give up anything else, *anything,* but I will not give up my love under any circumstances"? When you can respond to this, you are very close to the reign of God.

- Read faith statement #22 again and reflect together on how the pathway of Jesus's journey has led to this very day and hour. How is his work now being done? How do we continue the work of healing and teaching and loving, the journey to the cross, and the resurrection to new life?

PART THREE **+ ARTICLES 541–556 OF THE CATECHISM**

Message

[28] The message of Jesus can be summed up in a single, major line. Vatican II's *Dogmatic Constitution on the Church* summarizes this in article 3: "To carry out the will of [God]," it says, "Christ inaugurated the kingdom of heaven on earth and revealed his mystery to us."

[29] Let us repeat that: *"Christ inaugurated the kingdom of heaven on earth."* And what does that kingdom look like? It has several hallmarks.

[30] First, Jesus began his work by forming a community of men and women in whose company he spent his life. That community, you might say, was an early form of the Church, and today it is continued in the Church to which we belong. The Church is not itself the reign of God, but it is a sign and a pathway to that reign.

Christ inaugurated the kingdom of heaven on earth. We now join him in working to bring that kingdom to fulfillment.

[31] Second, it was a hallmark of Jesus' ministry that we must die in order to live, that we must be last in order to be first, that we must love our enemies, and that we must give away our money to the poor. He turned so-called conventional "wisdom" on its head! This is the "paschal mystery," and anyone who desires the reign of God must be living this mystery every day.

[32] Third, life in this kingdom, it seems, is offered to everyone. This is no club for those who never sin; it's not some association of the like-minded, not one religious sect among many sects. No, this is the *reign of God* and it is open to all God's children, to all the People of God.

[33] Fourth (and this gets more challenging as we go), this kingdom apparently belongs to the poor. Again in this message Jesus is offering a revolutionary turnabout of so-called conventional wisdom. This is no small thing in the gospels.

[34] Time and again, the poor are cited as recipients of Jesus' message. In his inaugural statement in Luke's gospel, chapter 4, verse 18, Jesus announces point blank that he will "bring good news to the

poor." They are the blessed ones, he says in Luke, chapter 6, verse 20 (and also in Matthew, chapter 5, verse 3), because the reign of God belongs to them.

[35] Half of the moral sayings of Jesus are a warning about the dangers of undue attachment to riches. *Half.* It would be easier, he tells us at one point, for a camel to pass through the "eye of a needle" than for a wealthy person to enter the kingdom of God.

[36] Fifth, and most amazingly, Jesus invites sinners to the table. The table of the Lord is not reserved only for those who behave themselves, it seems. It is not a reward for being righteous or lawful, or even moral and just. He invites sinners to conversion, to take on love in their lives, but he also offers them boundless mercy.

[37] Implicit in all of this, of course, is this little idea: that to gain the kingdom you must give up everything else. And when you do that, all is given to you. Using parables as a teaching device, Jesus helps us gradually see that it is, indeed, as he has said: a mystery.

[38] Dying leads to life; poverty leads to the kingdom; light is stronger than darkness; and love is stronger than hate. One can only "see" this from inside the kingdom, it seems. To anyone else, this appears foolish. Yet another mystery: the kingdom is not something to be studied but a way of life to be lived. If you let go of your own security and take on the way of Christ, you will wake up one day and lo! you'll find yourself in the heart of the God.

[39] Sixth, once you give yourself to Christ and enter into the dying and rising of your own journey of paschal mystery, there will be signs in your life that will amaze you! So it was for those in Jesus' own time: people were healed by his word, and they were freed from hunger, injustice, illness, and death.

[40] His mission was to free us from slavery, that is, from a self-taking lifestyle that is not our God-given destiny. Once freed from sin like that, we become leaven in bread, salt for the soup, and light for the world.

[41] And finally, seventh, who has the keys to this kingdom? We must remember that the gospels were written long after Jesus' own death. The writers were struggling with how to understand their own roles in this kingdom now entrusted to them. Looking back they searched for clues and tried to recall Jesus' words and deeds. Slowly they organized themselves to worship, teach, and welcome new followers.

[42] We are always careful not to read the gospels too literally or fundamentally. They aren't intended as a roadmap but as a theological reflection to help us meet the needs of our day. What the gospel demands of us, in other words, is not yet fully revealed to us.

[43] As the early Church searched for an understanding of authority, they remembered that Peter was the one Christ had chosen. Weak himself and often confused about what things meant, unable to remain faithful during Jesus' trial, yes, *that* Peter. To him alone had Jesus given the keys to the kingdom.

[44] Jesus had called him a rock and named him first among the twelve. Today, that ministry of Peter is continued in the papacy, and the ministry of the twelve is continued by the bishops.

[45] But even though we have the pope and bishops, Christ is the head of the body, the Church. Church leaders stand "in the place of Christ" as they lead the Church. To know Christ, in fact, is to know his community, just as it had been during his own lifetime.

Group or personal process

- Consider the seven hallmarks of the reign of God. For each of them, reflect on how it influences your daily walk with Christ and the Church.

- Reread faith statements #30–34 aloud and talk about how God's kingdom is being established in your home, neighborhood, and nation. Who is called to work in this kingdom?

Prayer

Christ, you provide an example for us of how to live in the paschal mystery. You now invite us to imitate you, take up our own cross, and become humble as you did. You invite us to become poor as you did and die to ourselves. By your grace and your grace alone we are able to live as your followers and become members of your body. We open our hearts now to you, Jesus, and invite you to seize us with your divine power of love. Amen.

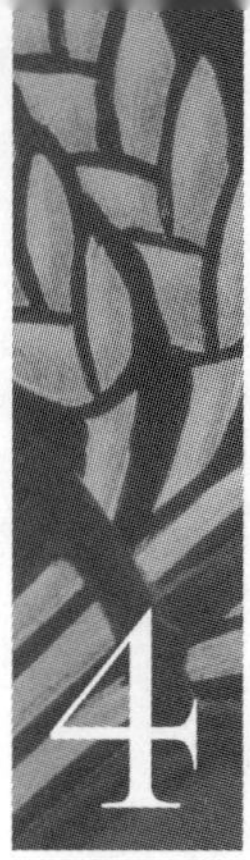

Session Four

THE PASSION OF CHRIST

BASED ON ARTICLES 557–560, 571–591, AND 595–618 OF THE *CATECHISM OF THE CATHOLIC CHURCH*. TO READ A SUMMARY OF THIS SECTION, SEE *CATECHISM* ARTICLES 592–594 AND 619–623

Introduction

Having now considered the person of Jesus Christ and the place of Mary, his mother, we turn to the crux of the story: the Passion of the Christ. We know that Jesus' was a prophetic voice that threatened the religious leaders of his day. He taught of love and mercy, of forgiveness and freedom. This threatened those who wished to impose a rigid law, and they opposed him. But even though some Jews of the first century were among those who opposed Jesus, the Jewish people and their descendants are not responsible for the death of Christ. Jesus gave us a tremendous sign of his love for us at the Last Supper when he washed the feet of his disciples and when, in the end, he freely offered himself for our salvation.

Scripture

READER: A reading from the Gospel of Mark.

Pilate spoke to them again, "Then what do you wish me to do with the man you call the King of the Jews?" They shouted back, "Crucify him!" Pilate asked them, "Why, what evil has he done?" But they shouted all the more, "Crucify him!" So Pilate, wishing to satisfy the crowd, released Barabbas for them; and after flogging Jesus, he handed him over to be crucified. (MARK 15:12–15)

READER: The word of the Lord

ALL: Thanks be to God.

ARTICLES 557–560 AND 571–591 AND 595–597 OF THE *CATECHISM*

The stage is set

[1] There had been no secret in Jerusalem that the authorities were pretty much fed up with Jesus. They wanted him off the streets. The deep motives will always remain fuzzy: Did they fear his power among the people? Did they have real problems with his theology, believing him to be a blasphemer? Were they looking for a scapegoat?

[2] Did they think Jesus was associated with some radical sect with real plans to overthrow the government? Were they jealous of Jesus' popularity, especially among the poor and lower classes? Was one of them, a leader maybe, gunning for promotion with Pilate? Did they fear he would incite the Romans against the local populace? Or had they heard his message and absorbed what he was saying about God but not dared to face it?

[3] Prophetic voices have always been an annoyance to official religious leaders; they challenge the status quo. Whatever the motives, Jesus seemed to know when it was his time to go up to Jerusalem. He "set his face" in that direction. The time had come.

[4] Luke gives a poignant and revealing detail about Jesus' own heart at this moment. As he was coming near the city of Jerusalem, Luke tells us in chapter 19, verse 41, Jesus wept over it. "If you, even you, had only recognized on this day the things that make for peace! But now they are hidden from your eyes."

[5] At the Liturgy of the Eucharist, when we sing those memorable words, "Blessed is he who comes in the name of the Lord!" we join our voices with the poor and common people of Jerusalem as Jesus entered the city for the last time. We must always remember that when the gospel writer put those words on the lips of the crowds, it was not so much to give a biographical note as to express the faith of the community of the writer!

[6] The gospels were written *after the resurrection,* which allows them to offer more a theology than a historical account. But the entry into Jerusalem was triumphant, as they told the story. Jesus had come home to the city he loved. It was the season of Passover.

The trial

[7] Public opinion about Jesus was sharply divided. Even among the highest rank of Jewish authorities were some who believed and some who misunderstood him. In the end, those who feared him and considered him a blasphemer and madman won the day. They handed him over to the Romans under the charge of political revolt.

[8] The Romans had a death penalty, as many uncivilized governments do, and Jesus was condemned under its rubric.

Who's responsible?

[9] There is always a temptation to blame someone when events turn
ugly. Down through the centuries, Christians have blamed Jews, all
Jews who ever lived, including those presently alive, for the death of
Christ. Then, having laid blame at their feet, Christians have killed
Jews or at least made them their enemies.

[10] It's true that the Gospel of John seems to vilify the Jews, but the
writer of this gospel had a particular goal and purpose. John's entire
account of the Passion is actually triumphant!

[11] There is promise in this death, according to John, that all who
believe will join him in the powerful presence of God. The focus of
this gospel is not on the tragedy of the cross but on the power of
God, and to read it as a condemnation of Jews is to misread it.

[12] The great decree from Vatican II addressing non-Christian
religions teaches clearly in article 4 that "neither all Jews indiscrim-
inately at that time, nor Jews today, can be charged with crimes committed during his passion."

Group or personal process

- Why do we humans tend to blame others when things go
  badly?

- Why do we blame God at times?

- Looking back over the material in this part of the lesson, tell
  the story of Jesus' Passion in your own words.

Changing our minds

[13] In fact, the goal of Jesus' life and death was to restore us humans to a proper relationship to God. Jesus' goal was not to "change God's mind"; nor was God's purpose to cause Jesus to suffer in order to be appeased. Jesus wanted to change our minds but it seems that we humans can be a hard lot to convince about God.

[14] Jesus spent his entire ministry helping us see God as near at hand and within our comprehension. Jesus spent his life on a campaign to change our thinking so we could see that God is merciful and kind, slow to anger and abounding in love.

WE BELIEVE

Our salvation flows from God's offer of love for us. Because he loved us, Christ restored us to love in God. Jesus freely offered himself to save us.

[15] In the end, for Jesus his mission did not appear very successful. He went to his death abandoned by his friends and feeling, at least in some accounts, as though perhaps even the Father in whom he fervently believed had let him down.

[16] But here in this setting Jesus reached deep into himself and found the divine source of love about which he preached. Empowered by the energy of never-ending love, he refused to despair and *refused to give up his love.*

[17] His vision remained steadfast: God is good, gracious, and trustworthy. In this sense God opens our eyes, our ears, and our hearts to common, ordinary, everyday love.

The mystery of his death

[18] In a mysterious way, Jesus' death fits into his ministry of struggling against false gods to help us understand who God really is. From the beginning, it seems, we humans have not understood this very well. We had grown to believe that God is angry or cruel, that God is distant from us, that we should fear God, that God punishes us, or that God does not love us.

[19] These are all images of the *false god* that Jesus corrects in his teaching. Our sin is believing in this false god. We are dealing here with a tremendous mystery: God is constant and has never changed. God loves us, period. Jesus the Son of God went to his cross in order to change *us*. What greater love could there be? What greater power?

What does this all mean?

[20] For more than two thousand years, Christians have been asking themselves this question. What does this mean for us? The Church has consistently taught that these mysterious first-century events were all part of how God would reach back into our lives. God our maker and source of life and love created us for paradise.

Group or personal process

- In your own words, what did Jesus accomplish through his suffering and death?

- Jesus' death opened the doorway to God's mercy and forgiveness to us. What is your experience of this compassionate God?

To set us free

[21] The First Letter of Peter lays out for us in clear terms what it means to be free. In chapter 1, verses 18–19, it says "You know that you were ransomed from the futile ways inherited from your ancestors, not with perishable things like silver and gold, but with the precious blood of Christ, like that of a lamb…"

[22] Jesus himself never believed in the "futile ways" of our ancestors, but he struggled against them with all his might in order to set us free. Free for what? To love, with the passion of the God who first loves us.

[23] Love for whom? For everyone. Jesus' focus was on the ministry that we have described here. With a thoughtful consciousness of his mission, Christ went about teaching, healing, and reintroducing people to God. In the final act of love, the one in which he laid down his life rather than surrender to hate and violence, a great breakthrough occurred.

[24] When he forgave his killers on the cross rather than surrender to their hate, he said, in essence, "Do you think that this can stop me from loving you? *Even this?*"

Supper

[25] Perhaps this divine love was made plainer in that final supper they shared. At table on the eve of his passion, Christ leaves his friends with a memorial. It was no complex, highly philosophical doctrinal system. It was not gilded vessels and silk vestments. It was not even a written Scripture or an organized church.

[26] It was a simple meal: "Do this in memory of me," he told them. Likewise, after the meal, he left them an example by washing their feet as a servant would do. Again, this is a simple but powerful gesture meant to teach us to serve one another.

WE BELIEVE

We are called to imitate Jesus and die to ourselves out of love for him and each other. Only when we die with him will we also rise with him.

The garden

[27] Then, as the story unfolds in all four of the gospel accounts, they went out to a garden to pray. Not an easy moment for Jesus, this scene brings to the fore for him that purpose and mission that was his and his alone: to set free the human race from the bondage of false gods.

[28] He accepts the mantel of this difficult journey because he sees that it is his purpose and, even though violent, the only way to restore our relationship with God. This sacrifice of Christ is unique; it completes and surpasses all other sacrifices.

[29] It is important for us who follow Christ to do what this man did. We must live with the faith that sustained him to his death, for this is what will set us free from darkness, fear, and sin. We must enter into our own "passover," our own exodus, our own movement from darkness to light, from being bound to being free, from fear to trust, and from hate to love.

[30] In this way, Jesus became our suffering servant and acted on behalf of us all. John's gospel sums this all up for us in a beautiful phrase in chapter 13, verse 1. "Having loved his own who were in the world, he loved them to the end," it says.

[31] Christ knew and loved us all in his dying and rising, for, as St. Paul wrote to the Corinthians in the second letter, chapter 5, verse 14, "the love of Christ urges us on because we are convinced that one has died for all, therefore, all have died."

[32] For us the mandate becomes clear: we too must take up our cross, and we must commit ourselves to *never give up our love* for any reason at any time even if it costs us our own very lives.

Group or personal process

- What are you called to die to in your life so that you can rise with Christ?

- What makes following Jesus' teaching so difficult for us? Why is it difficult to love our enemies, give generously to those who ask of us, and forgive seventy times seven times?

- Describe what life in your parish, neighborhood, or society would be like if everyone lived as true disciples?

Prayer

Jesus, you humbled yourself and took the form of a slave, being born in human likeness. You humbly suffered and carried your cross to open for us the encounter with love. You never gave up your love, even though it cost you your life, and you teach us to do the same. Now we turn our hearts to you. In the quiet of our souls, we listen intently for your word, your call, and your grace. May your word confront us in our sins, comfort us with your mercy, and empower us to become your hands and feet in today's world. Amen.

Session Five

BASED ON ARTICLES 624–628, 631–635, 638–655, 659–664, AND 668–679 OF THE *CATECHISM OF THE CATHOLIC CHURCH*. TO READ A SUMMARY OF THIS SECTION, SEE *CATECHISM* ARTICLES 629–630, 636–637, 656–658, 665–667, AND 680–682

Introduction

Well, of course, we have already heard the end of this story, and it did not end at the tomb. We ourselves experience Christ living among us and empowering us through grace, and the early followers of Christ also experienced him alive among them after his death. They were the first to know him as risen Lord. They especially experienced him while sharing meals together, creating the solidarity and community they had known during his public ministry among them. Now in baptism, we enter into the death of the Lord in order to enter also into his resurrection. In this sense, we join with those first disciples and with men and women from all the ages since. We believe that Christ lives now in the heart of God from whence he came and opens for us the way to that divine heart.

Scripture

READER: A reading from the Gospel of Luke.

But on the first day of the week, at early dawn, they came to the tomb, taking the spices that they had prepared. They found the stone rolled away from the tomb, but when they went in, they did not find the body. While they were perplexed about this, suddenly two men in dazzling clothes stood beside them. The women were terrified and bowed their faces to the ground, but the men said to them, "Why do you look for the living among the dead? He is not here, but has risen." (LUKE 24:1–5)

READER: The word of the Lord.

ALL: Thanks be to God.

PART ONE ✣ **ARTICLES 624–628 AND 631–635 OF THE *CATECHISM***

He is dead

[1] We believe that Jesus died that day, crucified among thieves, hanging on that cross. He died and was buried in a local tomb. This brings us to the Easter Vigil in the liturgical life of the Church, to Holy Saturday night where we celebrate the mystery of this death leading to new life.

[2] There is a sense of waiting between the events of Good Friday and those of Saturday night. We celebrate the Vigil remembering and retelling our long story of salvation history; we bless new water and new fire; and we glory in the resurrection of Christ!

[3] For us Christians, this leads to baptism, celebrated as the high point of the Easter Vigil. For in baptism we ourselves die in Christ and we go into the water, into the tomb, to emerge as men and women recreated in Christ. The great mystery of the tomb and our great faith in the communion of saints together with our experience of God restoring us from selfishness and sin lead us to believe that all the dead know the Christ.

[4] That one anointed by God touches all holy women and men dead or alive, which is why we pray in our Creed, "He descended into hell; on the third day rose again…"

He is raised

[5] We turn to some of the earliest Christian writings, to the letters of Paul, to grasp the understanding of the Church about the Resurrection of Christ. "I handed on to you," Paul wrote to Corinth, "as of first importance what I in turn had received: that Christ died for our sins…that he was buried…that he was raised on the third day…that he appeared to Cephas…"

[6] This early faith provides the basis for our own. Paul did not himself witness these events, but he learned of them after his own conversion. The stories were told in the community and repeated and repeated and repeated. Now they are handed on to us. "Why do you look for the living among the dead?" the women had been asked in Luke, chapter 24, verse 5, reflecting the faith of the gospels.

WE BELIEVE

Having died and conquered death and evil, Christ rose from the dead and lives among us as risen Lord. The early disciples encountered him.

[7] No one had been an eyewitness to the resurrection; indeed, all they suspected at first was a missing corpse. And, remember, the gospel writers wrote their accounts some forty years later—forty years of being Church, of commemorating that morning hour when they first encountered the risen Lord.

[8] Their account provides us with the theology that peers into this

great mystery but does not really explain it. We believe in the resurrection because of their early belief but also because we ourselves know Christ the risen Lord in our midst today.

[9] The women disciples were the first to encounter Christ but not as they had during his lifetime; Christ appeared to them in his glorious, powerful presence, a spiritual body, according to St. Paul. They told the men, including Peter and the others. The faith of the first community was established. He is raised!

Group or personal process

- Have you had an experience of the risen Christ in your own life? Share it.

- When you have given of yourself lovingly and generously, dying to yourself in the process, how do you experience resurrection as a result?

- What happens when you put others first, when you forgive easily, when you turn your heart to Christ in prayer, and when you share your faith with others?

PART TWO **+ ARTICLES 638–655 OF THE CATECHISM**

The risen Christ

[10] Try to imagine what this experience must have been like for those early believers. He had been seized from their midst, tortured in public as they hid, and killed like a common criminal.

[11] He had been the one in whom they had placed all their hope and faith, the one who had been teacher to them; he had been companion and friend. They'd never experienced anyone quite like this man, Jesus. They understood his principle very well: never give up your love, *never*.

[12] But they could not have imagined that he would give even his life for us. They understood so little, and perhaps we too understand too little. For we cling to life, to possessions, to power and position and prestige. We forget that God, in the end, is stronger than hate, darkness, and fear, and that love is more important than everything else.

The experience of the risen Lord

[13] They began experiencing him again: in the context of a meal at Emmaus, or a fish fry on the beach in John's gospel, or in that upper room among the twelve, or, as Paul reported, to "more than five hundred...at one time" in 1 Corinthians, chapter 15, verse 6.

[14] Here he is among them in his "glorious body" no longer limited by time and space, transcending all they could understand. We are not talking here about a corpse that has been resuscitated, as happened to Jairus' daughter, the son of that widow of Naim, or Jesus' friend Lazarus.

[15] Resurrection is not a return to earthly life, but it is a new way of being. Those who experienced him knew Christ now as filled with the Holy Spirit and sharing even more fully in divine life. Most of those who experienced the risen Christ had been his faithful followers but in the end had also abandoned or denied him.

[16] Their community was fractured and dispersed, and they were hiding for fear that they too would be asked to choose between God and their lives! So then, after the dark night of this moment passed over to the dawn of reunion with each other, perhaps they gathered in a shared meal, perhaps at a warm fire, in an embrace, or with a comforting word from Mary or John.

[17] And there, in that renewed solidarity, in that recommitment to his love, in that assembly of Christ's own, lo! he is there among them again! It's no accident that many of the experiences of the risen Christ occurred in the context of meals. Where else? For Christ's own memorial of his saving death and resurrection had been a meal, after all.

[18] And for us Christians, the meal became *Agape*, a Greek word that means "sacred love" celebrated in a "love feast." It became Eucharist, which means "Thanksgiving." Each time we share this sacred meal, each time we assemble for Eucharist, even just two or three of us, Christ is present among us as he promised.

[19] The experience of the risen Christ is that experience on which our faith is based. It completes and seals and confirms all he taught and all he did during his years of ministry. In the reality of the resurrection flows a river of new life that fulfills a promise made in ancient times. We have been set free from that human inclination to selfishness, and we have also been offered a pathway to new life.

[20] We are returned to the power of God through grace. We are empowered now to forgive endlessly, to love with passion, to help the materially poor, and to be generous, inclusive, and just. Truly, this is victory over death!

[21] For we are now sisters and brothers; we are sons and daughters of God. We have a real share in the life of Christ, risen and present. The promise is immense: in Christ we shall all arise. When we put on Christ as a garment, in Paul's words, or when we give over our own hearts, we live no longer for ourselves, but for Christ…Amen.

Group or personal process

- In what contexts do you have your most powerful experiences of the risen Christ? With whom do you experience solidarity, community, and unity?

- Talk about some recent wonderful meals you have shared with others. Don't focus only on holidays or birthdays, but think about ordinary meals.

- What hope do you take away from learning the teaching in faith statement #21?

PART THREE ✛ **ARTICLES 659–664 AND 668–679 OF THE CATE-CHISM**

He is ascended!

[22] There is a very touching story in chapter 20 of the Gospel of John. Mary Magdalene, who has been among the closest of Jesus' friends and

companions, is standing outside his tomb, weeping. Her loss had been immense and she had remained with him to the bitter end.

[23] While she wept, the text tells us, two angels engaged her, and while they talked, Jesus appeared but did not reveal himself. But when he uttered her name, Mary! she recognized him in an instant! Then he told her, "Do not hold on to me because I have not yet ascended to the Father..."

WE BELIEVE

Christ's ascension marks the definitive entrance of Jesus' humanity into the heavenly place. From this we receive grace and power through the Holy Spirit in order to build the reign of God.

[24] We must be careful not to treat our belief in the Ascension too literally. Christ certainly lives now in God; indeed, Christ *is God in our midst*; he is the Son of God living among us. But heaven is not out beyond the stars or up above the earth, so even though we use the term "Ascension," we do not mean to suggest "a going up" in any physical way to any physical place.

[25] When we become too literal, we lose the beautiful meaning of this very real experience of Christ to which his early followers testify. Leading the way for us, Christ, who is now the risen Lord, returns to the intimacy of God. Just as Jesus was the Son of God born to Mary and Joseph, teaching, healing, and walking with us, so now the risen Christ resides in the same God.

[26] We must connect our understanding of Christ ascending with Jesus' teachings on the reign of God. Recall that the mission of Jesus was to inaugurate the reign of God among us. In this he re-

stored us to divine life and reconciled us to the Father. The final and most powerful expression of this reconciliation is found in the Ascension, when Christ makes it possible for us all to know God intimately.

He comes again!

[27] Christ is not absent from us at all! He lives now in the Church, the body of Christ, and the community of faith. The Church growing in faith and love is a sign of the reign of God to the entire world. And yet...we believe he will come again.

[28] By this we do not mean that we believe Christ will be born again of Mary or preach and teach again in Galilee. No, much more powerfully, we mean we believe Christ will one day reign with love and grace and light over all darkness.

WE BELIEVE

Christ already reigns through the Church. We are in movement toward ever greater light, toward the day when all darkness will be overcome by him.

[29] The reign of God is already present, we say, but not yet *fully* present. We await the day when it will be complete. We Christians believe that when we die, the love we have in our hearts is what we take with us for eternity.

[30] We believe that we will be judged based on our conduct, on the purity of our motives, and on the secrets of our hearts. Chapter 25 of Matthew's gospel echoes the whole Christian tradition when it warns that we will be asked whether we fed the hungry. Did we

clothe the naked, visit the prisoner, and welcome the stranger?

[31] Our attitudes toward our neighbor, the patterns of our lives, will clearly show whether we accepted grace, or refused it. Then it will be known what we did to the least of Christ's little ones.

[32] We long to hear those words from Matthew's gospel, "Come, you that are blessed by my Father, inherit the kingdom prepared for you from the foundation of the world…"

Group or personal process

- How do you connect all the aspects of Christ's paschal mystery for yourself: dying to self in love for others, rising to new life in love with Christ, and going forth to love and serve every day?

- What concrete actions and practices can you undertake to help build the reign of God and to participate in the movement toward a world of love, peace, and justice?

- Read faith statement #29; how do you see the reign of God present today?

Prayer

Jesus, when you spoke her name to your friend and follower Mary Magdalene, she recognized you. Speak our name to us now. Let us listen within our hearts to hear it: Martha, Bill, and John, Dan, Therese, Mark, and Jean…it is I, the Lord. I am with you. I walk with you each day. I know you and love you. I choose you as my own. I am your shepherd and you are my sheep. I am the vine and you are the branches. I am in you and you are in me. Amen.

Session Six

SOCIETY AND HUMAN DIGNITY

BASED ON ARTICLES 1877–1889, 1897–1917, AND 1928–1942 OF THE *CATECHISM OF THE CATHOLIC CHURCH*. TO READ A SUMMARY OF THIS SECTION, SEE *CATECHISM* ARTICLES 1890–1896, 1918–1927, AND 1943–1948

Introduction

We have learned about the birth, family, ministry, passion, and resurrection of Christ. But in order to understand what difference this makes, we turn now to two topics that make that plain. First, in this session, we will learn about how we are called to live together in society. We could also say "live together in the reign of God" because there is a connection between the unity of the Trinity and the community that we humans are called to establish among ourselves. Society, we believe, ought to promote the exercise of virtue and not obstruct it. Society, in fact, should be organized around a sense of value and the common good of all. Public authority in such a society is exercised legitimately only if it is committed to the common good of all. To attain this, it must employ morally acceptable means. The equal dignity of human persons requires the effort to reduce excessive social and economic inequalities.

Scripture

READER: A reading from the Letter of James.

What good is it, my brothers and sisters, if you say you have faith but do not have works? Can faith save you? If a brother or sister is naked and lacks daily food, and one of you says to them, "Go in peace; keep warm and eat your fill," and yet you do not supply their bodily needs, what is the good of that? So faith by itself, if it has no works, is dead. (JAMES 2:14–17)

READER: The word of the Lord.

ALL: Thanks be to God.

PART ONE ✦ **ARTICLES 1877–1886 OF THE** *CATECHISM*

Society

[1] Each of us is called to be God's image in the world and to animate the world with the Spirit of Christ. But it is also true that humanity as a whole has this lofty calling. All people are called to live together in the same shared life that we find in the union of the Triune God.

[2] Hence, love of neighbor is inseparable from love for God. Living together with our neighbors is not incidental to our lives. It is part and parcel of who we are as human beings. We are not set side by side collectively, but we are bound together by a principle of unity beyond any one of us.

[3] We gather in societies. The societies in which we live are not of our making but are something we receive from our forbearers and likewise pass on to those after us. We owe a certain debt to these societies. We owe loyalty to one another as we all seek to advance the "common good."

[4] No matter what society we live in, we humans must always be the

principle, the subject, and the end. Certain societies such as family and state are necessary in order for us humans to survive. Other more voluntary societies also help us by providing a platform from which to reach our social goals: economic, recreational, professional, and political. Such societies also create their own dangers if they limit personal freedom or initiative.

The human person needs life in society, reflecting life in the Trinity, in order to develop as God intends. Therefore, participation in groups and associations that support the common good is encouraged.

[5] The Church follows a principle regarding this: "subsidiarity." This principle teaches that central authorities should not interfere with local societies without serious purpose and cause. For example, the government should not interfere with family life. Rather, central authorities should support local societies, help them when needed, and coordinate everything for the common good.

[6] We believe, therefore, that neither the state nor any larger society ought to impose itself on individuals, families, or local communities. Nor should such larger societies substitute themselves for the initiative and the responsibility of individuals or smaller groups.

Common values

[7] Being in society is essential to the fulfillment of our human vocation. Because of this, we Catholics consider the interior, spiritual dimension of human life on a par with the exterior, physical dimension. That is, spirituality and social interaction are of equal value

because society is the place where men and women share knowledge, exercise their civic rights, and are inspired to live by their values.

[8] Society is the place where men and women derive genuine pleasure from beauty, music, theater, nature, and art. Here too is where we follow a common law in an orderly society with value-driven economics and politics.

[9] Society is where we share the "spiritual" dimension with one another in order to lift our spirits and make our shared life nobler.

[10] We believe it is up to us, as members of a universal Church and as citizens of a global society, to advance the cause of justice and to change institutions that fail to honor human dignity or help to make evident the spiritual dimension.

[11] For this we depend on grace, on God's self-communication to us. We need the help of the virtues, especially courage, wisdom, and charity, lest we surrender to evil as cowards or become violent ourselves in an effort to end violence! Charity, indeed, is the greatest social commandment because it leads us to respect others, to seek justice and human rights for all, and to sacrifice ourselves for the common good.

Group or personal process

- What is the relationship between church and society?

- What role do you play in education, the arts, business, recreation, or commercial activity that can be made to support the rights of the poor and the good of all?

- We are the Church, and we are also part of many societies at local, state or provincial, and national levels. How do we bridge the two?

Authority

[12] In 1963, Saint John XXIII wrote about peace on earth in an encyclical entitled, in Latin, *Pacem in Terris*. "Human society," he wrote in the encyclical, "can be neither well-ordered nor prosperous unless it has some people invested with legitimate authority to preserve its institutions and to devote themselves as far as is necessary to work and care for the good of all."

[13] Every human society, in other words, whether a family or a nation, needs authority to govern it. This is just simply part of human nature. Such authority flows in the final analysis from God alone. This is ancient Christian teaching deriving from St. Paul.

[14] Good order in society requires that all obey the laws. We believe this is God's plan for how we are to live. The obedience we are bound to give authority should be rooted in respect for leaders and motivated by gratitude and good will, provided the leaders are just and deserve such respect.

[15] It is because such authority flows from God's own plan for us that the choice of who should rule any society belongs solely to the free decisions of the citizens of that society and to no one else. Hence, governments do not derive their authority from themselves, and they must always follow natural law, seek public order, and defend the rights of all.

[16] They may never behave as despots or dictators and may never take away from the people their political rights of freedom and responsibility. Public authority is legitimate only when it seeks the common good of those being ruled and if it uses moral means to do that.

[17] When a government makes laws that are immoral, one is not obliged to obey them. Power within a government is balanced by other powers within that government, one group governing the other, as it were. This results in a principle known as "the rule of law," where just laws are honored and followed rather than the arbitrary will of the citizens. Well-ordered and safe society results.

The common good

[18] We believe that the good of each individual is closely connected to the common good and dependent on it. Hence, we must all participate in seeking the common good. When we use the term "common good," we refer to the sum of social conditions that allow people, either as a group or as individuals, to live full lives and seek happiness.

[19] We cannot reach human fulfillment alone, hiding from each other in fear, isolated and independent, each seeking only what he or she needs without regard to the community. The common good concerns the life of all and has three essential components.

[20] First, the common good is based on respecting the human dignity and freedom of all persons. Each person should be allowed to follow that vocation that sounds in his or her heart, calling them to this or that work in life. Each must be allowed to follow his or her conscience, for example, and to have privacy, freedom to worship, and so forth.

[21] Second, the common good is based on the development of the group itself. The highest duty of society is to provide the basic needs for all: food, clothing, homes, health care, work, education, culture, honest information, and the right to establish a family.

[22] Finally, the common good requires peace, resulting in security and a just social order. Morally acceptable means must be used to achieve this, however. We do have the right to legitimate collective defense but only as a last resort. It is the role of the state to defend and promote the common good of society.

[23] In today's world, we also must seek the common good of the family of nations, paying special attention to the poor, to refugees, migrants, and those in misery. As a world community, we employ the United Nations to provide a forum for dialogue and negotiation, as a way for small nations to be heard, and as a way to protect human rights.

Group or personal process

- How do we shape moral and just societies? What role do you play in this process?

- Why is it in the interest of the Church to guard and protect a social order that allows for freedom and peace?

- When would it be justifiable for a Christian to disobey a civil law? Name such a law and say why it can be disobeyed.

PART THREE ✦ **ARTICLES 1897–1917 AND 1928–1942 OF THE** *CATECHISM*

Participation

[24] Each of us is called to participate in society according to our position and role, and such participation is inherent to our dignity. The first level of this is taking charge of personal needs: the education of one's family, meaningful work, caring for one's property, and so forth.

[25] The second level is working in public life to shape society, demanding honesty and accountability, staying informed on social matters, and promoting humane conditions of life.

Social justice

[26] Society makes sure that social justice is a reality by providing those conditions that allow individuals or groups to obtain their due. Social justice is absolutely rooted in human dignity. Society exists for the benefit of persons, not persons for the welfare of society.

[27] Respect for human dignity is respect for rights. And human rights flow from our dignity as sons and daughters of God. When rights are respected and freedom is honored, society remains well ordered, but when rights are flouted and ignored, only force and violence maintain order, and humans suffer indignity.

[28] The Church often reminds people of good will about these rights. Each of us should look upon our neighbor as "another self," treating them as we want to be treated. This is based in charity not legislation. This means we must care especially for those who suffer, the disadvantaged, the rejected, and the materially poor.

[29] But it applies as well to those who think differently and who live or act differently from us. We must end prejudice and promote tolerance and deep appreciation for our many cultures.

Equality

[30] All men and women everywhere share a common origin: we are all made by God, and we all share a deep spiritual bond. We all share in the same human dignity, no matter what culture or background, no matter which gender, race, or color, no matter what social setting, language, or religion we may practice.

[31] We need each other from our first moments of life, and throughout our lives we depend on each other. Even though we are

different from one another, it is the sum of our talents and cultures that makes up the rich human family. One has this gift, another has that gift, and, taken together, we have all the gifts we need.

[32] Therefore, we must eradicate material poverty and eliminate the awful inequalities that exist throughout the world. These inequalities are the root of war and violence because they do not result in the common good which is the only avenue to peace.

Solidarity

[33] We are called by our Christian heritage to seek the solidarity of the human family throughout the world. In the first place this means we must distribute the goods of the earth with more fairness. We must pay everyone who works a fair wage, no matter where they live. We must seek just laws in every nation and reduce tensions by negotiation not by war.

[34] We must resolve economic disparities by uniting workers, by bringing rich and poor together, by urging employers to be just, and by encouraging solidarity among nations. Indeed, world peace depends mainly on this. We are also encouraged to share our spirituality and blessings of faith, opening avenues of respect and love.

Group or personal process

- How can we establish social justice in the world today? What is needed in the hearts of people? What is needed in their governments?

- How do various political parties and viewpoints prevent us as a society from reaching these social goals? Read faith statements #30–33 again and talk about each right in your own society. Why is it being achieved or why not?

Prayer

O God, you have called us to live together as your family. You have given us the earth and all its goods and asked us to share them among all your children. And you have renewed our hearts by continually offering a covenant to us. Now fill us with your Spirit so that we may fulfill this destiny and live as you desire. Create new hearts in us, hearts full of mercy for those who suffer, and hearts full of compassion for the poor. May the society we create as your children reflect the goodness of your own heart. We pray through Christ, our Lord. Amen.

Session Seven

GRACE AND MERIT

BASED ON ARTICLES 1949–1974 AND 1987–2016 OF THE
CATECHISM OF THE CATHOLIC CHURCH. TO READ A SUMMARY OF THIS
SECTION, SEE *CATECHISM* ARTICLES 1975–1986 AND 2017–2029

Introduction

How can we create the kind of society described in the last session? Only through grace and shared community is this possible. We have working for us, of course, the reality of grace. What we seek for society is within what we call "natural law." The natural law flows from our participation in God's wisdom and goodness. It expresses the dignity of the human person and forms the basis of our fundamental rights and duties. It is rooted in the grace of the Holy Spirit received in Christ; it is expressed in the words of the gospels; it is celebrated in the sacraments.

Moved by grace, we turn toward God and away from selfishness and sin, and this movement is called "conversion." Grace is the help God gives us to help us become God's own children, intimately connected to the love of the Trinity.

Scripture

READER: A reading from the Letter to the Philippians.

Therefore, my beloved, just as you have always obeyed me, not only in my presence, but much more now in my absence, work out your own salvation with fear and trembling; for it is God who is at work in you, enabling you both to will and to work for his good pleasure. (**Philippians 2:12–13**)

READER: The word of the Lord.

ALL: Thanks be to God.

The law

[1] We Christians follow a moral law that is the work of divine Wisdom. Biblically, the law is like parents instructing their children on how to grow up and live in happiness and avoid those evil things that cause unhappiness and ungodliness.

[2] We believe that we are created according to a certain holy order that we can apprehend and understand. Following this created order is the pathway for us to being whole and fulfilled as humans. This divine, eternal law is written into our very hearts!

[3] There are several different kinds of law and all of them are related to each other: eternal law, natural law, revealed law, civil law, and church law. All of this talk of laws ends in Christ, who is in himself an expression of them all.

Natural law

[4] We are all endowed with a marvelous gift, which is to be able to discern truth from falsehood. From the beginning we've had this ability, and it is what distinguishes us from animals. We call this inner voice "natural law" because it was implanted by the Creator

and is a sort of "original moral sense." We call this law "natural" not in reference to the nature of beings, but because it is part and parcel of human nature.

[5] If we follow this law, we will be fulfilled because it leads always to what God desires. St. Thomas Aquinas sums this up for us like this: "The natural law is nothing other than the light of understanding placed in us by God; through it we know what we must do and what we must avoid. God has given this light or law at the creation."

The law is a parental instruction from God that helps us find the way to true inner peace and happiness, to human fulfillment.

[6] Natural law provides the whole human race with certain common principles even though application of the law varies greatly according to culture and circumstance. Natural law itself does not change, because it is written into our very hearts. It may be expressed by a variety of rules and may fit into custom and changing ideas, but it always remains substantially valid.

[7] It is the foundation on which we build society, including the moral rules that govern us and keep us in good order. It's the foundation of the human community, and from it rises all civil law. We do not always see and understand natural law immediately and clearly without the help of grace and revelation.

The Old Law

[8] The laws articulated in the Old Testament evolved as the people of God did. Through prophets and teachers, this law gradually came

to express the call to do justice, which is rooted in the human heart.

[9] The Old Testament law is summed up in the Ten Commandments. In short, these commandments urge us to do what is loving and to avoid what is not. As such, they enlighten our consciences so that we can hear God's voice, discern it amid the chatter of other voices, and follow it. This law was articulated so clearly through Moses because we failed to read it in our hearts. Christian tradition sees these commandments as holy, spiritual, and good but as incomplete because they tell us what to do but do not give us the grace to do it.

Group or personal process

- What are some of the "natural laws" that are stated in the Ten Commandments? How has the human race progressed in following these? How have you personally done so?

- How do you hear the voice of God echoing in the depths of your soul and directing you to avoid evil and do what is good?

PART TWO ✛ **ARTICLES 1966–1974 AND 1987–1995 OF THE CATECHISM**

The New Law

[10] The New Law works through charity and is founded in grace. Grace is God communicating God's own self to us through the Holy Spirit, who is given to the faithful in Christ. One might say that this new law is summed up in the teachings of Christ, especially the Sermon on the Mount in Matthew and the Sermon on the Plain in Luke.

[11] This New Law might, in fact, be called "The Law of the Gospel." In his teaching, Christ surpasses the Old Law and brings it to perfection, orienting us all toward the kingdom of heaven. It is addressed to those most open to this new hope: the poor, the humble, the rejected, the sinner, the afflicted, the pure in heart, and the peacemaker. To these are given the secret of the reign of God.

[12] The New Law seeks to reform the heart, the root of our actions as humans, where faith, hope, and charity are formed. By teaching us to forgive our enemies, this new law teaches us to be like God. In the New Law we are taught to practice our religion for God to see, not for other men and women to see.

[13] Indeed, the entire law of the gospel is contained in the "new commandment" of Jesus to love one another as he has loved us. All of this is slightly less juridical and slightly more pastoral than the Old Law. Under the teachings of Christ and those of Paul and the apostles, we are animated by charity, not by the letter of the law.

[14] One can actually be keeping the letter of the law, according to Christ, but still not be keeping the New Law. How does one measure the heart? How do we judge love?

[15] The New Law is called a "law of love" because it wants us to act with love rather than out of fear. It is called a "law of grace" because it gives us the power to act, which the Old Law did not do. It is called a "law of freedom" because it leads to truth, the truth that

makes us free. This New Law sets us free also from the ritual and legal practices of the Old Law and leads instead to spontaneous acts of love. The New Law is lived in charity: love of God and neighbor.

Justification

[16] We are united to Christ by baptism. In baptism we gain a share in Christ's victory over selfishness and sinfulness. In our everyday lives we die in Christ and we are born to love in a new life. This is the New Law.

[17] All of this occurs through grace, which is experienced as a divine energy or power helping us become what we are created to be. Grace helps us sin less. We call this grace which comes from the Spirit by a name: "justification." We have the power given to us by Christ with which we can become loving, with which we can overcome selfishness and sin, and with which we can enter into community.

[18] Indeed, the very first work of grace is to turn our hearts to Christ, helping us "fall in love" with God; and the second work of grace is to help us accept the mercy and forgiveness of God.

[19] Hence, we are purified in our hearts and reconciled to the gospel and each other. God, of course, has always been "waiting" and has never left us. It is through his own dying and rising that Christ prepares us for this saving moment.

[20] We humbly accept the divine offer of love and reconcile ourselves to God's pathway. This reconnection is possible because of Christ, who brings together God's grace and our freedom. This is the most excellent work of God's love that we see in Christ and that is empowered by the Holy Spirit.

Group or personal process

- What is your own experience of being justified or reconciled to God, your neighbor, and even to your own self?

- Read faith statement #17 again and share about how you have experienced the "power" of grace at various key moments of your life.

- How do you understand the connections between the Old and New Laws?

Grace

[21] Grace is a free gift that is experienced as a divine, loving power that helps us respond to God's call and to become sons and daughters of God. It is participation in the life of the Triune God: in baptism we enter into the death of Christ and become an adopted "child of God" through the power of the Holy Spirit.

[22] We cannot fathom why God would love us so much or how deep that love is. And yet grace is being given to us, flowing like a river of Spirit: free, undeserved, healing, and powerful. "Therefore," Paul wrote to the Corinthians, "if anyone is in Christ, there is a new creation; everything old has passed away. See, everything has become new. All this is from God, who reconciled us to himself through Christ."

[23] Sanctifying grace is this ongoing presence of God within us,

forming and shaping us at all times, drawing us ever more into the divine heart.

[24] Grace is free, indeed, but we must respond to it; and we are free to do that or not to do it. Grace responds to the deepest yearnings of our hearts, implanted there by God, the yearning for love and divine blessing. God both gives us this gift and moves us to receive it. Grace comes to us under several forms or experiences, all under the power of the Spirit.

WE BELIEVE

Grace is the help God gives us to respond to our calling and become his adopted daughters and sons. Grace introduces us to the intimacy of life in the Trinity.

[25] We receive special graces through the sacraments, and each of them in its own way deepens our love. We receive special graces of "charism" or gift meant to build up the Church, each person receiving gifts appropriate to him or her.

[26] Grace, in short, is a free gift from a loving God, a share in God's own life, making it possible for us to live in Christ. No one can "corner the market" on grace because it is such a mysterious and divine power. How do we know when we have it or when we don't? This may be the wrong question. Rather, we learn to trust that God is with us and look to see the fruits of grace.

[27] St. Joan of Arc was asked by the Church judges who were trying to trap her if she knew that she was in God's grace. She is said to have replied, "If I am not, may it please God to put me in it. If I am, may it please God to keep me there."

[28] God has given us everything we have, as a father or mother does for their child. In a sense, we deserve none of it: creation itself, hearts made for love, the gift of friendship and companionship, the lovely pleasures of life, our faith and the turning of our hearts, and even the sufferings that come our way.

[29] It is all free gift. And yet God continually loves us, forgives us, and draws us back to each other. So anything we might claim is ours is really God's in the first place. Only when we are moved by charity and the Spirit do we turn our hearts to God, and only then do we live as God's children. The charity of Christ is the source in us of all our merits before God.

The call to holiness

[30] We are all called to holiness, to the fullness of the Christian life, and to perfect charity. This is not a calling reserved for priests and religious but is something each baptized person has implanted within them.

[31] The pathway to holiness is love lived day in and day out. And the only way to love like this, we know, is to pass by way of the cross, to die to selfishness within ourselves, and so to rise in love with Christ. This entails a spiritual battle, a way of life aimed at holiness.

Group or personal process

- What is your experience of grace? How do you feel "empowered" by God?

- What gifts have you received for the building up of the Church?

- Read faith statements #30 and 31 again. Describe the often-circuitous pathway to holiness that you have followed in your life. What people supported you, what special moments were there, and what turning points did you experience along the way?

Prayer

O God, you have written a law of love upon our hearts, and your voice now echoes in the depths of our souls, calling us to do what is good and to avoid evil. By your grace alone are we able to hear that voice, and by the power of the Holy Spirit we are able to respond with love. We now turn once again to you and offer you our hearts and hands for the work of your kingdom. Fill us with the power of your love, we pray through Christ, our Lord. Amen.